Published by **Lost Alphabet**

With offices at:
1603 Capitol Ave. Cheyenne, WY, 82001
United States of America

www.lostalphabet.com

Curated by Michael Washienko

ISBN-13: 978-1-948333-02-3

Library of Congress Cataloging in Publication data available upon request

NO PLACE LIKE HOME

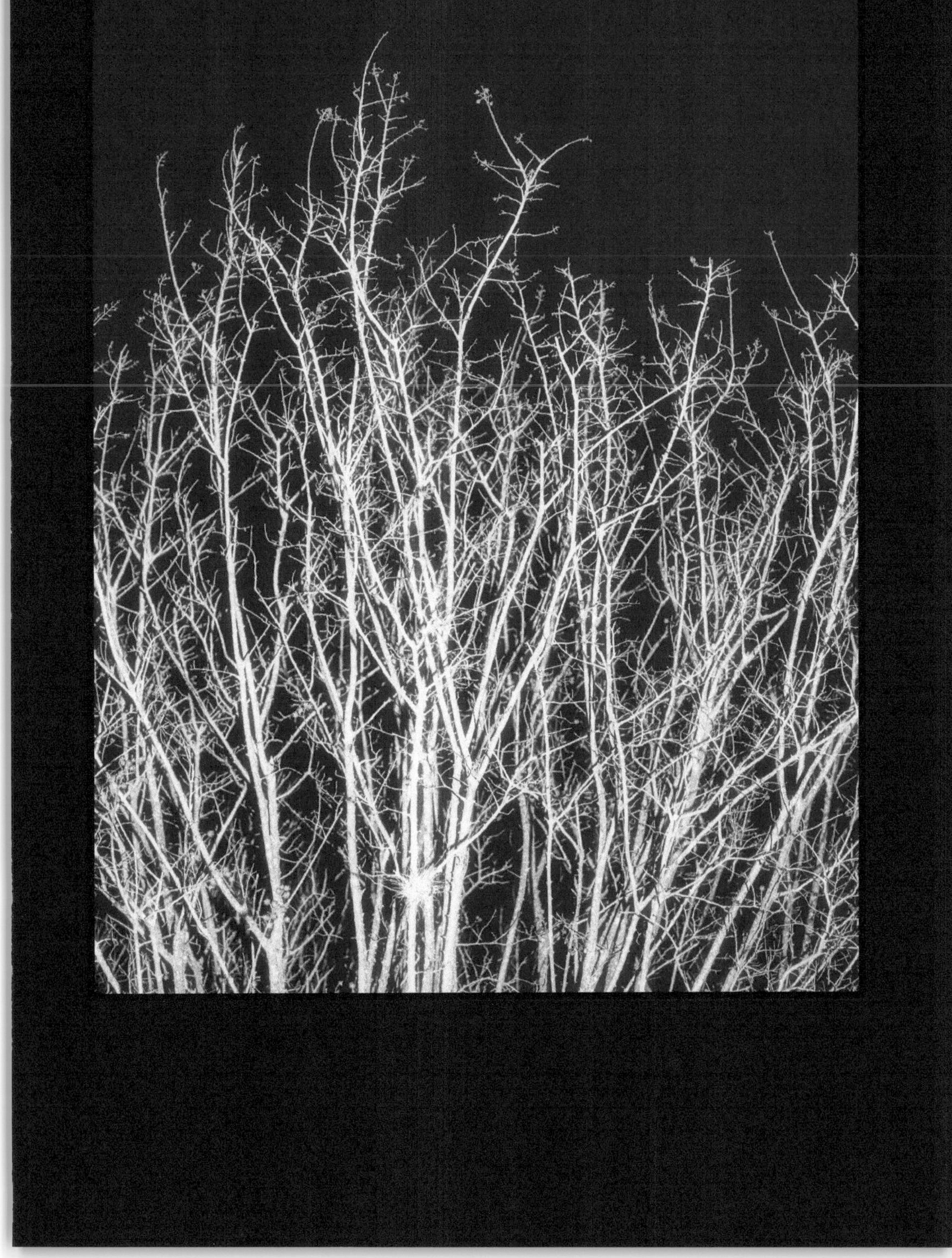

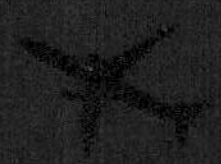

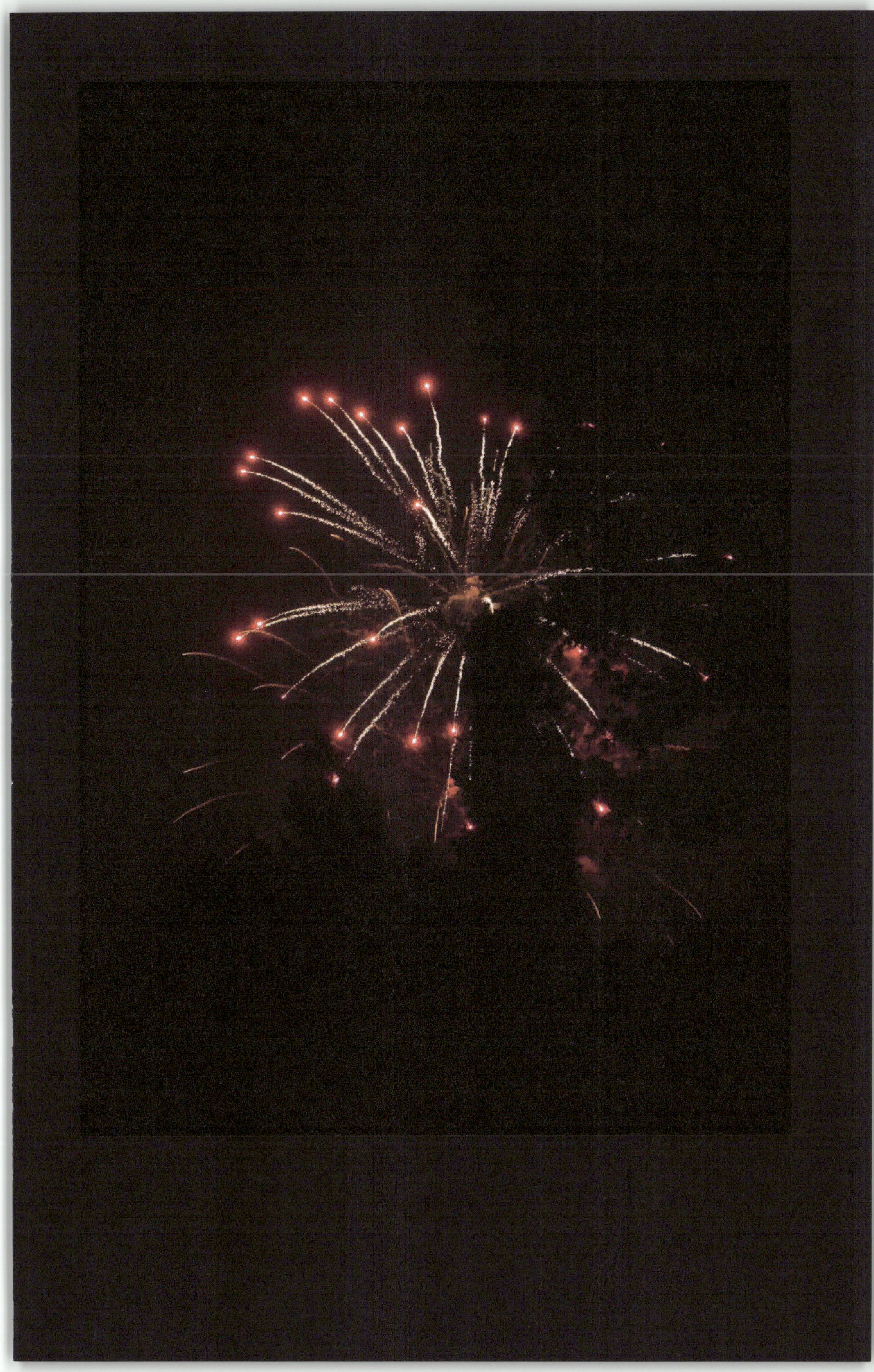

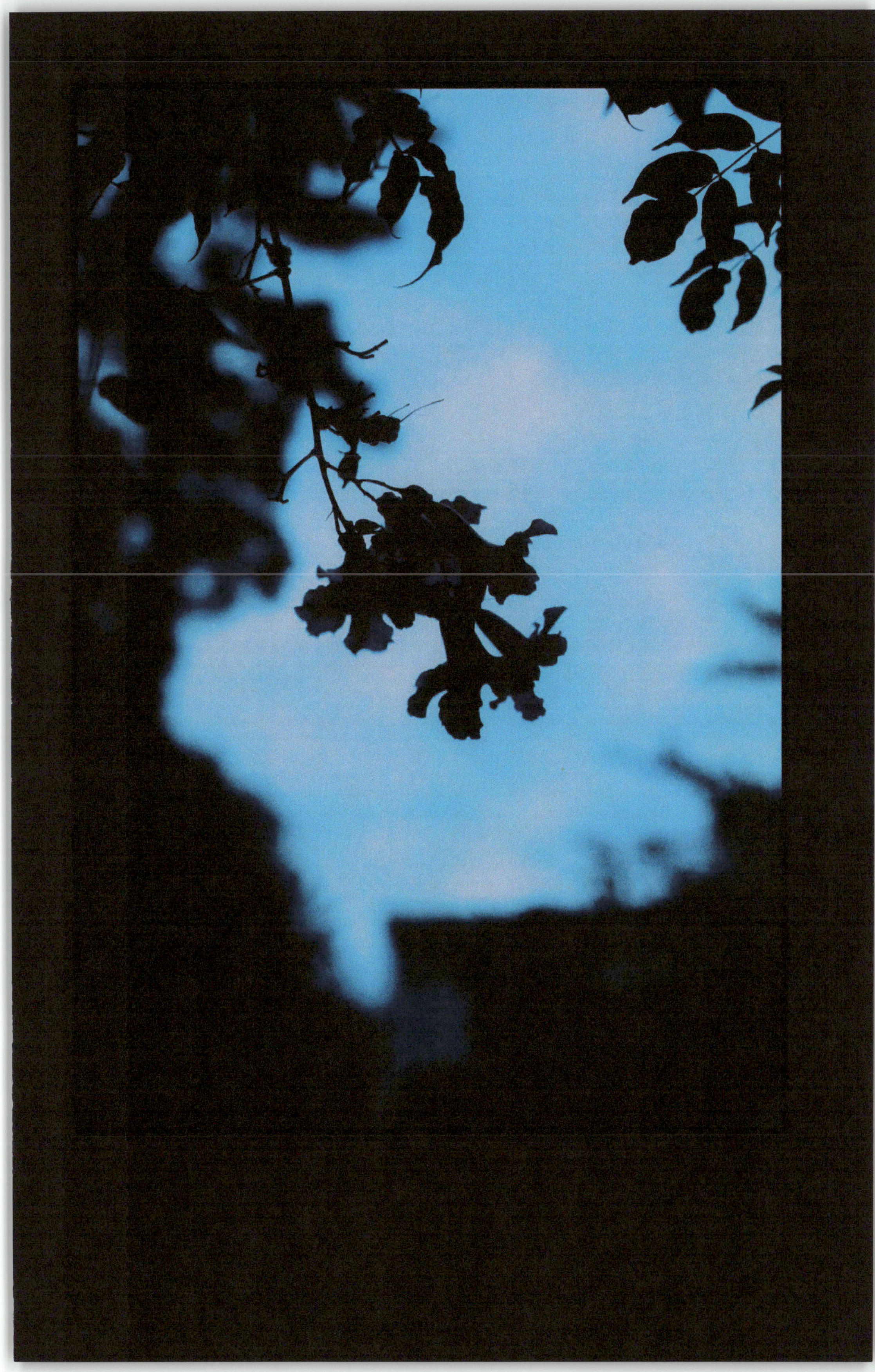

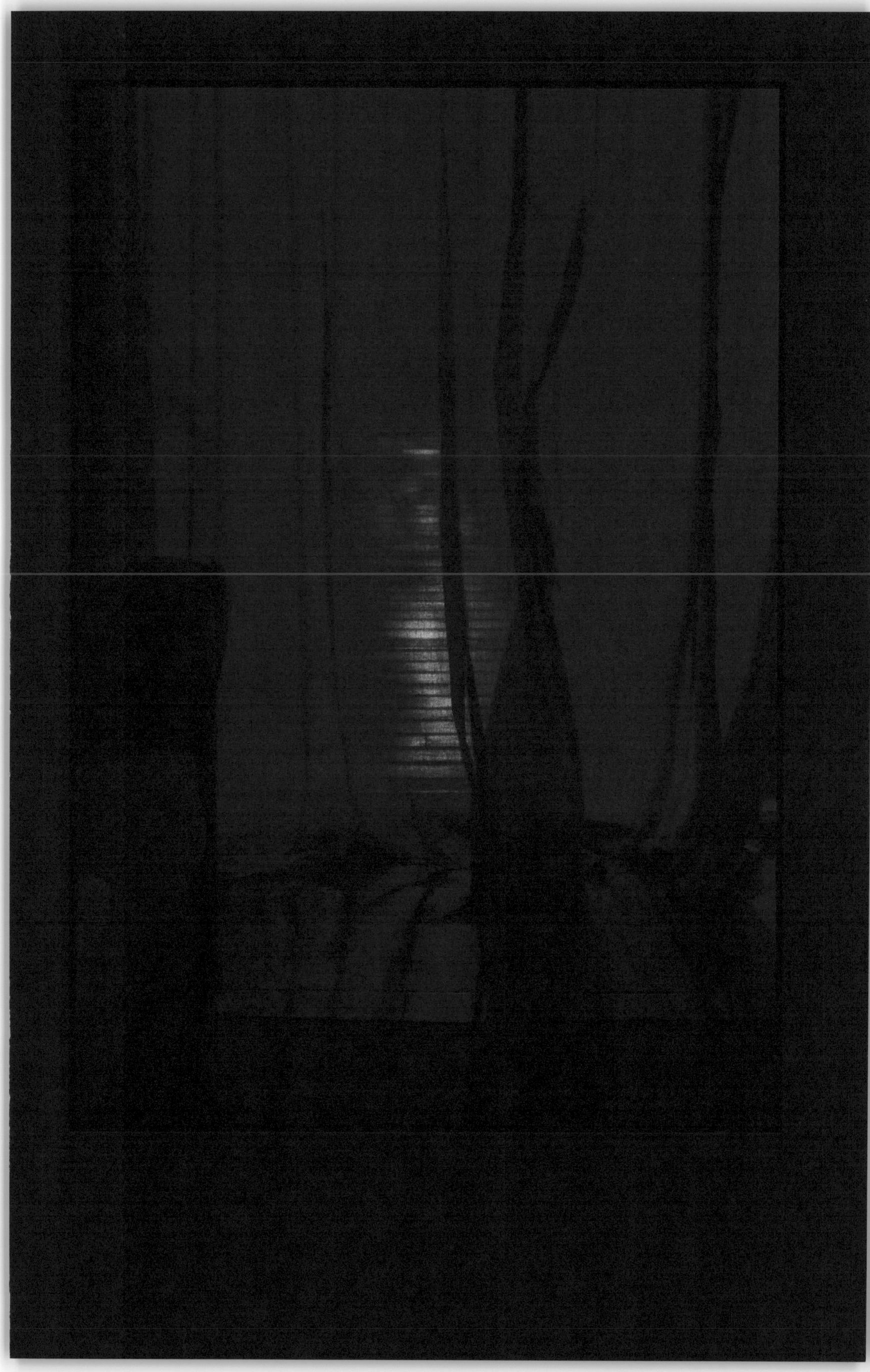

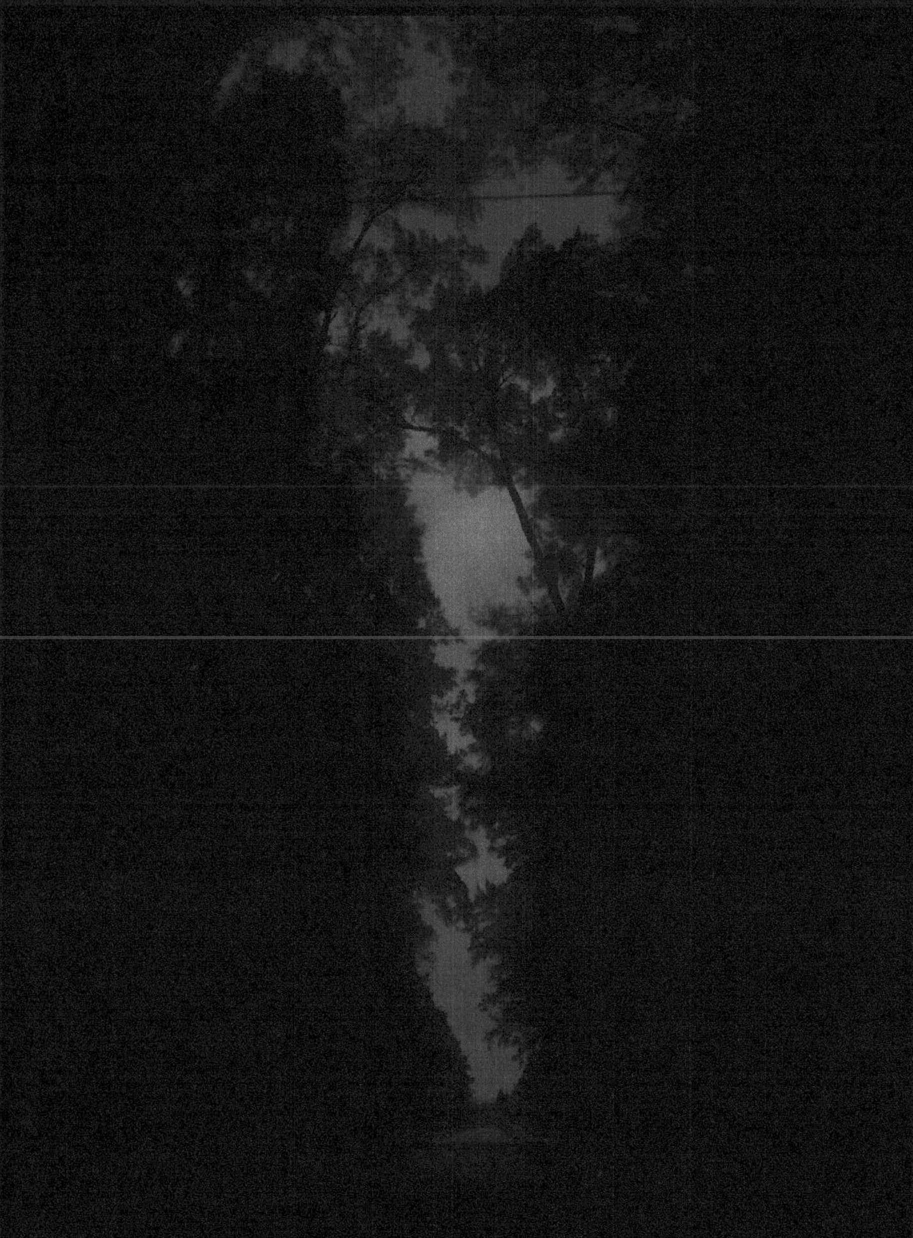

No Place Like Home is a series of loosely connected images that explore the theme of nostophobia (the fear of returning home), shot between 2016 and 2018 in Buenos Aires.

Lost Alphabet

www.ingramcontent.com/pod-product-compliance
Lightning Source LLC
Chambersburg PA
CBHW040331220526
45473CB00009B/2643
9781948333023